4 2539 00011 8494

W9-CCV-946

WITHDRAWN

Return to
CHILDREN'S ROOM
F. H. COSSITT LIBRARY

The Kids
Book
of Golf

John
Gordon

Property of the
TOWN OF GRANBY, CONN.
F. H. COSSITT LIBRARY

WITHDRAWN
Return to
CHILDREN'S ROOM
F. H. COSSITT LIBRARY

Kids Can Press

Dedication
To William, Alexandra and Maggie: This is YOUR Kids Book of Golf!

Acknowledgments

To the golfing kids who helped with this book: my children, Will, Allie and Maggie; Alexa, Anna and Ava Loiskandl; Shaun and Jaimie Ironstone; Mike DiCarli, Jacqueline Yates, Andrew Thoms, Kristen Irvine, Rebecca Smith, and the senior classes at Monsignor Castex School in Midland, Ontario, Canada. I apologize if your picture or other input didn't make it into the book, but without you this project wouldn't be nearly as good. Thanks!

To my friend Doug Ball, a great photographer who does it for the love of the game.

To Paul MacDonald of the Royal Canadian Golf Association for his friendship, guidance and access to the Future Links materials, and to Karen Hewson of the Canadian Golf Museum and Hall of Fame for access to the archives of photos.

To Tiger Woods for strapping booster rockets to the greatest golf boom the sport has ever known.

And, most sincerely, to my wife and partner, Leslie, for her motivation, inspiration and perspiration in helping me produce this manuscript. — J.G.

Future Links images and instructional material in this publication have been provided by Future Links, Canada's National Junior Development Program. Future Links is a partnership of the Royal Canadian Golf Association, Canadian Professional Golfers' Association and Provincial Golf Associations. Future Links information can be obtained by contacting the Royal Canadian Golf Association at 1-800-263-0009 or www.future-links.org.

Text © 2001 John Gordon

All rights reserved. No part of this publication may be reproduced, stored in a retrieval system or transmitted, in any form or by any means, without the prior written permission of Kids Can Press Ltd. or, in case of photocopying or other reprographic copying, a license from CANCOPY (Canadian Copyright Licensing Agency), 1 Yonge Street, Suite 1900, Toronto, ON, M5E 1E5.

Many of the designations used by manufacturers and sellers to distinguish their products are claimed as trademarks. Where those designations appear in this book and Kids Can Press Ltd. was aware of a trademark claim, the designations have been printed in initial capital letters.

Neither the Publisher nor the Author shall be liable for any damage that may be caused or sustained as a result of conducting any of the activities in this book without specifically following instructions, conducting the activities without proper supervision, or ignoring the cautions contained in the book.

Kids Can Press acknowledges the financial support of the Ontario Arts Council, the Canada Council for the Arts and the Government of Canada, through the BPIDP, for our publishing activity.

Published in Canada by
Kids Can Press Ltd.
29 Birch Avenue
Toronto, ON M4V 1E2

Published in the U.S. by
Kids Can Press Ltd.
2250 Military Road
Tonawanda, NY 14150

Edited by Laurie Wark
Designed by Julia Naimska
Printed in Hong Kong by Wing King Tong Company Limited

The hardcover edition of this book is smyth sewn casebound.
The paperback edition of this book is limp sewn with a drawn-on cover.

CM 01 0 9 8 7 6 5 4 3 2 1
CM PA 01 0 9 8 7 6 5 4 3 2 1

Canadian Cataloguing in Publication Data

Gordon, John, 1952 May 23 –
        The kids book of golf
Includes index.
ISBN 1-55337-017-1 (bound)   ISBN 1-55074-617-0 (pbk.)
1. Golf — Juvenile literature. I. Title.
GV968.G67 2001   j796.352   C00-931843-7

NELVANA

Kids Can Press is a Nelvana company

Contents

Introduction

Imagine that the calendar has rolled back hundreds of years, and you and your friends are shepherds in Scotland. It's a sunny afternoon, the sheep are grazing and you have nothing to do. You swing your crook at a round stone. The stone rolls along the ground and into a rabbit's hole. Way to go — you just invented golf! And you got a hole in one!

Okay, so it might not have happened quite like that, but experts say it could have. The game we know as golf has been around in one form or another for many centuries. It is now one of the world's most popular sports.

Golf is a game you can play your whole life. You can start when you are very young and continue for the rest of your life. Golf pro Tiger Woods began playing when he was 2 years old. Amateur golfer Erna Ross got a hole in one when she was 95.

Another great thing about golf is that it's a friendly game. You can play with a few friends or you can go to a course by yourself and meet new friends. And because there are golf courses all over the world, you can make friends wherever you go.

Golf is also a game for people of all sizes and abilities — you don't have to be big or strong to play well. It's more important to hit the ball straight than to hit it far. A good swing will make the ball go a long distance and in the right direction. If you keep it on the fairway, you can get the ball into the hole without too many strokes. And the fewer strokes you take in golf, the better.

GOLF TALK
If you see a golf word you don't understand, check the Golf Talk glossary on page 44.

Drop your weapons – let's golf

 About 500 years ago, golf was so popular in Scotland that the king commanded everyone to stop playing. He thought his subjects were golfing instead of practicing archery and other war skills needed to defend Scotland against attack. But about 10 years later, the king started to play golf himself. He liked it so much that he declared it a game for everyone. And he let them play again.

People have discovered very old paintings of people playing a game that looks similar to golf in France, Italy, England, the Netherlands and Japan. Some people say golf began in the Netherlands, where a game called "kolf" was played as long ago as 1297. One theory is that when Dutch sailors went to Scotland, they took their kolf clubs and balls with them. The Scots went so crazy over the game that they started to believe that they had invented it themselves. Whether it is true or not, Scotland has the honor of being called the home of golf.

Caddy Willie, painting by C.H. Robertson, circa 1839

CARRY YOUR BAGS, SIR?

A caddie is a person who carries a player's golf bag around the course. Professional golfers are about the only people who use caddies anymore. But before golf carts were invented, most golfers hired caddies to carry their clubs. The word "caddie" likely came from the French word cadet, or young man. That's what the French golfers in the 1500s called the boys who carried their clubs.

Every pro, like Ernie Els, has a caddie.

The golf course

Golf is played on a specially designed piece of land called a golf course, which is usually divided into nine or eighteen different areas called holes. A game, or round, of golf begins on the teeing ground of the first hole. The teeing ground is an area of short grass with markers to show you where to hit from.

Each time you hit the ball with your club, you count one stroke. At the end of each hole there is another area of short grass, called the green. On the green, there is a small hole. The idea is to get your ball from the teeing ground into that little hole on the green in the fewest strokes possible. The area between the teeing ground and the green is called the fairway. The grass on the fairway is shorter than the rough, which is on each side of the fairway. You may also find yourself among trees or bushes, in shallow holes filled with sand called bunkers, or even in a pond or a stream.

Glen Abbey Golf Course, Ontario, Canada

Golf holes

There are three kinds of golf holes on most courses: par threes, par fours and par fives. Par threes are the shortest and good players are expected to hit their ball onto the green from the tee in one shot. On par fours, it should take a good player two shots, and three shots on par fives.

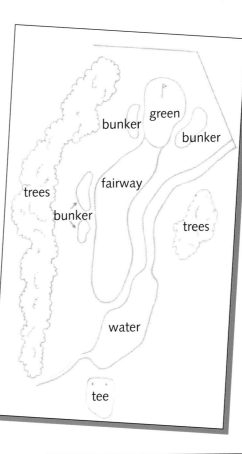

green

bunker

bunker

fairway

trees

bunker

trees

water

tee

Par three

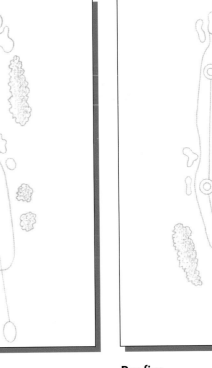

Par four

Par five

The clubs

Mashie, baffie, niblick and spoon — sound more like things you'd see on the dinner table than on the golf course. But when golf professionals made their own clubs, they got to pick names for their creations. Now that clubs are made with space-age technology and numbered 1 to 9, it's much easier to remember which club is which.

Some clubs are best for hitting the ball a long way. Others are better for shorter shots. The rules of golf say you can carry no more than 14 clubs in your golf bag, but you don't need a full set of clubs when you start out. A 3-wood, 5- and 7-irons, and a putter are enough to begin. Clubs should be fitted to your height. You can usually have them cut to the right length at a golf course pro shop.

At least three clubs are called woods even though they are probably made of metal or another non-wood material. The longest club is the No.1 wood, called the driver. It is used for hitting the ball off the tee. The other woods, usually a 3-wood or a 5-wood, are mostly used for hitting the ball when it is on the fairway.

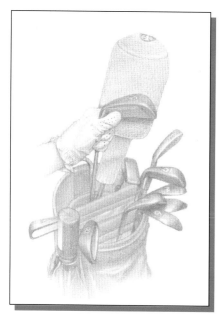

The irons are the clubs with smaller heads, used for hitting shorter distances. Your set may have any or all of the following irons: 1, 2, 3, 4, 5, 6, 7, 8, 9, pitching wedge and sand wedge. The higher the club's number, the shorter the distance the ball will go.

The pitching wedge is used to hit the ball high but not too far. The sand wedge is good for getting the ball out of a bunker, or sand trap.

Late 1890s rut iron

Wooden driver, circa 1915

The putter is used on the green to get the ball into the hole. Get a light putter that is not too long for you because you need to be accurate on the green to sink your putts.

WHEN IS A WOOD NOT WOOD?

Long ago, each golf club was handmade by a master craftsperson. Most of the shafts were made from hickory wood, while the heads could be made of wood or iron.

Steel shafts replaced wood in the early 1900s, but it wasn't until the 1970s that golf technology changed dramatically. Thanks to scientific advances, clubs can be made out of graphite, boron, Kevlar, ceramic or any sort of metal alloy. These materials make the clubs strong, light and durable. They may even help the ball go farther.

Rake iron (replica)

Other equipment

Now that you've got your clubs, you need a golf bag to put them in. Choose a small, light bag. Make sure there are a couple of good-sized pockets in it and that it has a comfortable shoulder strap. Some bags have double straps so you can carry them like a knapsack. Some have short legs that fold out to keep the bag off the ground. You can get bags with all kinds of features, but remember that these extras make the bag heavier.

Dressed to play

Just as you must have the right equipment to play golf, you should also dress properly. Most courses require golfers to wear a shirt that has a collar, pants (but no jeans) or shorts that are not too short, socks and shoes. While there are golf shoes with rubber-spiked soles, running shoes work almost as well, except in wet conditions. If you have metal-spiked golf shoes, call the club you are visiting to see if they are allowed. Many courses will allow only soft (non-metal) spikes.

Use one pocket of your bag to store golf balls, tees, a pencil, a ball marker and a ball-mark repair tool. Use a larger pocket to store a rain jacket. Don't forget sunscreen!

A small towel with a ring that attaches to your bag is handy for wiping your hands or cleaning dirt and water off the club or ball. And bring an umbrella if it looks like rain.

Golf balls

Like any new golfer, you will lose a few balls when you start out. Buy the cheapest balls you can find at a golf shop, department store or pro shop. These may be used balls that other golfers have lost on the course, but don't worry — they usually travel just as far and straight as new balls.

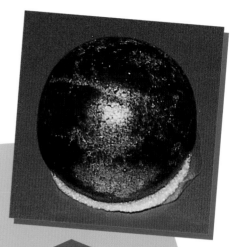

Feathery golf ball, circa 1840

Smooth gutta-percha golf ball, circa 1850

ROLLING THROUGH HISTORY

Some of the first golf balls were made by stuffing wet feathers into a pouch made of animal skin. The pouch was sewn closed and shaped into a ball. In a few days, the feathers would dry and expand, and the ball would be ready for play. The feathery ball was the only ball available for many years.

Then in 1848, a man in Scotland received a gift from India that was packed in gutta-percha, a rubberlike substance. He discovered that the rubbery packing could be shaped into great golf balls. These "guttie" balls were easier and cheaper to make than the feathery balls.

In 1898, a ball with a rubber core was invented. It was called the Haskell after its inventor. It could travel farther than other balls and didn't cost much to make. Today's golf balls are based on this ball.

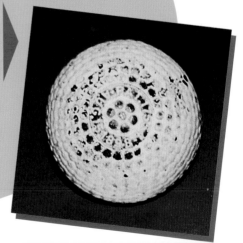

Early rubber-core golf ball, circa 1898

Bramble gutta-percha golf ball, circa 1880

Grip, aim and posture

Whether you are driving the ball down the fairway or sinking a short putt, each time you swing at the ball it counts as one stroke on your score. It pays to learn the right swing for each shot. You need a good grip, aim and posture to build a good golf swing — and become a good golfer.

The grip

The easiest grip to use is the ten-finger, or baseball, grip. For right-handed golfers, lay the grip of the club in your left hand along your fingers, a little higher than where they meet your palm. Move your right hand into position below the left the same way. You should be gripping with your fingers only. Your left thumb should be slightly on the right of the club, with your right thumb partially covering it and slightly on the club's left. Your hands should touch each other.

Left-handed golfers do the same thing but using the opposite hands. So, lay the grip of the club in your right hand above where your fingers meet your palm. Move your left hand into position below the right.

There are two other popular grips — the interlocking and the overlapping. In the interlocking, the index finger of the hand lowest on the club goes snugly between the pinky and ring fingers of the higher hand. In the overlapping, the pinky finger of the higher hand sits snugly in between the index finger and the middle finger of the lower hand.

The interlocking grip

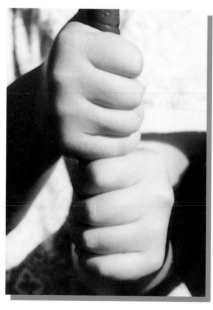
The ten-finger, or baseball, grip

The overlapping grip

Aim and posture

Aim is part of the address, or beginning position, of your swing. It is also called alignment. If you want to hit the ball straight to the target, you must have everything, not just the face of the club, aimed at that target. Your shoulders, hips and feet must be on a straight line. Imagine that railway tracks run from your right shoulder, through your left and to the target. (If you are a left-handed golfer, the tracks would start on your left and run through your right.) Your club head should be aimed down one side of the track and your body should be aimed the same way down the other side of the track. Your back should be straight, your knees slightly bent and your chin out. It's important to have good balance in your swing, so place your feet about shoulder width apart for a stable foundation.

STRANGE BUT TRUE

Pro golfer Jimmy Stewart was playing in India when he saw a huge cobra heading toward him. He killed it with a single blow of his 1-iron. Incredibly, another cobra slithered out of the dead snake's mouth. Stewart killed the second snake and was relieved when no other snake came out of its mouth!

Putting and chipping

On these pages, you'll learn about the short shots — putting and chipping. On the next pages you'll learn the full swing. (These instructions are written for right-handers. If you are left-handed, you can usually just reverse the directions.)

Putting

"Drive for show, putt for dough" is an old saying that means you can win or lose a game by being a good putter. Every stroke, whether a long drive or a short putt, counts toward your final score. It's easy to learn how to putt, but it takes practice to become good at it.

The putting grip is a little different from your usual grip. Place your left hand on the grip of the putter, then your right. The palms of your hands should face each other. Slide your right hand a little lower than the left. Your thumbs should be visible down the front of the club. Hold the putter lightly.

Place your feet about shoulder width apart and point your toes straight out. Slightly bend your knees. Put the putter midway between your feet. The club face should almost touch the ball and point directly at the hole.

Keep your body and head steady. Take a good look at the hole. Imagine rolling the ball with your hand into the hole. Then look at the ball and bring the putter straight back, still thinking about how hard or soft you would roll the ball to get it into the hole. Without taking your eyes off the ball, stroke it smoothly toward the hole.

The putting grip

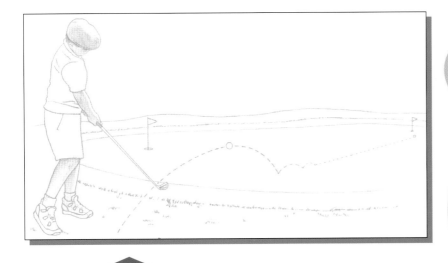

STRANGE BUT TRUE

In 1932, a golfer in Mexico City hit a great shot that stopped just short of the hole. As he was about to putt, an earthquake hit and the ball dropped into the hole for an ace!

Chipping

You chip the ball when it has landed close to the green but not on it. Chipping lets you hit the ball into the air over longer grass (the rough), so it lands on the green and rolls close to the hole. Try to get the ball as close to the hole as possible so you can use your putter on the next shot. Who knows? You may even chip the ball right into the hole!

Good clubs for chipping are the 7- and 9-irons. Hold the club the same way you hold the putter. Your thumbs are on top of the grip and your toes point straight ahead of you. But this time, put more weight on the foot closest to the hole. Move your arms back and forth. Try to brush the grass with your club as you make the stroke.

The full swing

When you take a full swing, remember that you'll have a better chance of making a good shot by keeping your swing smooth — not hard and fast. Watching golf tournaments on TV is a great way to see what a good golf swing looks like.

In the full swing, your feet are about shoulder width apart. The back foot — the foot farthest from the hole — points straight out from your body. The front foot is turned slightly toward the hole. Keeping your back straight, bend your knees a little, bend forward at the hips and stick out your behind slightly, as if you are about to sit on a high stool.

Hold the club lightly but firmly. Begin your swing by bringing the club back smoothly — low and slow — this is called the backswing. As you swing the club back, most of your weight should transfer to your back foot. Now sweep the club through the ball. As you do this, your weight will move with the club and end up on your front foot.

After you hit the ball, keep the club moving until your hands are in the air over your shoulder. This is called the finish position. Hold this position until the ball stops rolling (so you'll know where to find it). When you are in the finish position, check that your weight is on your front foot and that your back foot is now turned toward the hole and up on tiptoes. Your thumbs should point away from the target over your shoulder.

TIME FOR TEE

If you can, go to a driving range to practice hitting the ball. If you want to use a backyard or other open space, you should buy plastic practice balls, which don't go as far as real golf balls. Start by hitting the ball with your higher irons — 9-iron and 7-iron — and work down through the numbers. Then move to your woods — 5-wood and 3-wood — and finally to your driver. Until you are more experienced, you should always practice hitting the balls off a tee. When you can hit well off a tee, try hitting off the grass. Don't be afraid to take a divot, or piece of turf, when you swing through. It shows that you are getting under the ball, which helps lift it into the air. Just be sure to put the divot back, so the grass will root again.

Se Ri Pak in finish position

Playing by the rules

 Would you believe that one of the official rule books for golf is almost 600 pages long? Don't worry. You won't have to read it. That book is used for professional tournaments, when there is a lot of money or a championship title at stake. If you are playing a friendly game, you just need to follow some basic rules.

Keeping score

You must count every swing you make, even if you miss the ball. If your ball goes into the water or trees, where it is impossible to hit, you count a penalty stroke. You then pick up the ball and move it to an open area, not closer to the hole, where you can hit it.

Teeing off

When you start each hole, your ball must be between the tee markers. It can't be in front of them or more than two club lengths behind them. If your ball falls off the tee before you swing, it doesn't count as a stroke. But if you swing at the ball and miss, it counts as one stroke.

On the fairway

You must hit your ball from where it lands, but it's okay to move a nearby leaf or branch as long as you don't move the ball. If the ball moves, you must count a two-stroke penalty. If your shot sends the ball out of bounds, bring it back to where you hit it from and add one penalty stroke to your score. If you can't find the ball, add a penalty stroke and go back to where you shot from and hit again.

You must hit the ball from where it lands. Jack Nicklaus has a tricky shot here.

On the green

The player farthest from the hole putts first. If you are worried your ball might hit another golfer's ball, ask that player to mark his or her ball. Otherwise, if you hit it, you'll get a two-stroke penalty. If you are hitting onto the green and your ball hits a ball already on the green, there is no penalty. Just place the first ball in a spot as close to where it was before your ball hit it.

Pull the flagstick out before the ball gets to the hole. If you are on the green and you don't remove the flag before sinking your putt, you must count a two-stroke penalty.

STRANGE BUT TRUE

Talk about monkeying around on the golf course! Players in the 1980 South African Open had problems teeing off on the eighth hole when six monkeys decided to have a wrestling match there.

On course for golf

More rules? Nope. Just a few dos and don'ts to help you — and the other golfers — enjoy your day at the course. Part of becoming a good golfer is learning the manners and customs, or etiquette, of golf.

• Always take your practice swing away from other people. Being hit by a golf club can cause a serious injury.

• To keep the game moving quickly, take only one practice swing.

• Be quiet and don't move while another player is hitting the ball. This includes the people you are playing with and the group ahead of you, if you are waiting to tee off.

• Be ready when it's your turn. Your group must keep moving to avoid a traffic jam forming behind you.

• When you hit, watch your ball until it stops so you know where to find it when it's your turn again. After everyone tees off, the person whose ball is farthest from the hole hits next — that way, no one will be standing in front of a golfer when he or she is hitting.

• If you are looking for a ball and the group behind you is waiting, move to the side and wave them through. If you haven't found your ball in five minutes, it's considered lost. You must hit another ball from the spot where you hit the previous shot. The rules say that the proper way to drop a ball is to hold your arm out straight at shoulder height and release the ball. You must play the ball where it comes to rest.

• If you hit out of a bunker, rake the sand carefully when done.

• If your ball makes a mark when it hits the green, use a ball-mark repair tool to fix it.

• If you take a divot when hitting the ball, replace it.

• When you finish putting, quickly replace the flag and move to the next tee before marking your score. That way, you won't hold up the golfers behind you.

LIGHTNING ON? GAME OFF!

Golf can be played in just about any weather, but never in thunderstorms. As soon as you hear thunder or see lightning, get off the golf course. Most courses sound a siren or horn when lightning is near, but don't wait until you hear the siren to head to the clubhouse. If you get caught on the course, stay away from high ground and tall trees. Lightning usually strikes tall objects and metal, so lay your clubs on the ground and move away from them.

Warming up

When they get to the golf course, pro golfers warm up and hit many practice balls on the driving range before they go to the first tee. Try to get to the course half an hour before your tee-off, so you have time to loosen your muscles.

On the driving range

If you can, hit a bucket of range balls. It's fun to pound every ball with the driver, but think about the game. Which clubs do you use the most? The irons and your putter. Which one do you use the least? Your driver. Practice first with the most-used clubs — the irons — then hit a few balls with your driver or 3-wood.

Swinging

Standing well away from everyone, take several slow practice swings with the club you will tee off with. When it's your turn to hit, use that same easy swing.

On the putting green

Now head for the practice putting green. Use only one or two balls — it's more like being on the golf course, and fewer balls are easier to keep track of if there are many people on the practice green. Drop your ball about 1 m (3 ft.) from a hole and try to make the putt. Practice from this distance a few times. Then move back a few steps and try to make the putt from this distance. Choose another hole and do the same thing.

Stretching

Just before your group tees off, do these three simple stretches. Cross one leg over the other and touch your toes. Repeat, crossing the other leg in front. Next, stand on one foot, bend the other leg and pull it behind you. Then do the other leg. Finally, turn your shoulder from side to side and reach around the other shoulder, patting yourself on the back.

Drills and tips

Even if you can't get to a golf course or driving range, you can still work on your swing. You don't even need a golf club for some of these drills. Practice them in front of a mirror so you can see what you're doing.

Putt putt

Putting is the only stroke you can practice indoors with a club. If you are allowed, practice on a carpeted floor. Use a round piece of paper about 10 cm (4 in.) across as a target — that's about the size of a golf hole. Line up your putt and, keeping your eye on the ball, try to hit it onto the paper or slightly past it. Count to five before you look where your ball stopped. This helps you keep your head down during the putt, which keeps your ball on target.

Hello there!

Pick a target. Get into your starting position and put your hands on your hips. Now turn your body so your belly button points directly at that target. It's like saying "hello" to the target. This gets your body used to the turning motion of the swing and ensures that your body is in the proper finish position.

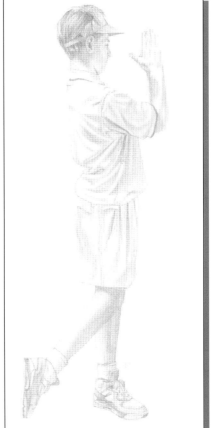

Thumbing around

Pick a target. Get into the starting position, with your arms hanging down. Put your palms together and point your fingers to the ground, but raise your thumbs up. Swing your arms back — turning your shoulders away from the target so your thumbs point at the target. Swing your arms toward your target. When you finish, your thumbs should be pointing over your shoulder, away from the target. This drill helps you develop a smooth — low and slow — swing.

Hey, waiter!

Get into your starting position. Place your left hand on your left hip. (Right hand if you are left-handed.) Hang your other hand in front of you with the thumb pointing out. Bring your hanging arm back like you would in a backswing, but stop at the top of the swing. Your palm should be level and facing the ceiling, as if you were a waiter carrying a tray high over your shoulder. Now swing, bringing your arm down and across your body and then up to pat

yourself on the back. This drill helps you properly position your hand, wrist and arm in the backswing and follow-through.

Games within the game

 There are many games you can play on a golf course. You can play some as a two-, three- or four-person team. This gives both new and experienced golfers a chance to play and practice together.

Scramble

This is a team game, usually with four players per team and any number of teams. Everyone on one team hits a shot from the tee. That team then picks the best tee shot, and all four players take their second shot from that position. This continues until one or more players from the team hits the ball onto the green. After selecting the easiest putt (usually the ball closest to the hole), everyone on the team takes a turn putting until someone sinks the ball. When someone does, the hole is over and you mark down your team score. Each team plays the same way.

Alternate shot

This game is for a two-person team using one ball. To begin, you make the tee shot on the first hole. When the ball lands, it's your partner's turn to hit the second shot using your ball. Then you hit from where that shot lands, your partner hits the next shot, and so on. You tee off on the odd-numbered holes (1, 3, 5, etc.), and your partner tees off on the even holes (2, 4, 6, etc.), no matter who putted out on the previous hole.

Quota points

In this game, you get points based on your score for each hole. You can create your own scoring system, but here's an example: 10 points for an eagle, 6 for a birdie, 4 for a par, 2 for a bogey, 1 for a double-bogey and 0 for a triple-bogey or higher. Using this system, if you shot a six on a par 5 (a bogey), you would earn 2 points. At the end of the round, the player with the most points wins the game.

The Yellowknife Golf Club at midnight

STRANGE BUT TRUE

If you live in the Far North, you can play golf 24 hours a day during the summer because the sun never sets. At the Yellowknife Golf Club in Canada, there is a tournament every year that starts at midnight.

Tips from the pros

Golf books, videos and computer games can help you improve your understanding of the game. So will these tips from some of the world's best players.

U.S. golf legend Jack Nicklaus was one of the first golfers to "waggle" his club — move it back and forth slightly — before he started his backswing. Jack believes that one of the worst things you can do is freeze like a statue when you are getting ready to hit the ball.

American pro Tiger Woods recommends the interlocking grip for players with small hands. In this grip, the right pinky finger intertwines with the left index finger (or vice versa for lefties). This helps your hands work together to make a better shot.

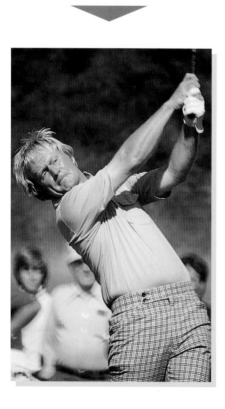

Sweden's Annika Sorenstam has different clubs in her bag than most golfers. Because she has trouble hitting with a 3-, 4- or 5-iron, she carries as many as five woods. To Annika, it doesn't matter what everybody else does; you must do what is right for yourself.

Mighty American golfer John Daly is the only golfer to average more than 300 yards per drive on the Professional Golfers' Association (PGA) Tour! John is also one of the fastest players. Playing quickly makes golf more fun.

Colin Montgomerie of Scotland was the best golfer on the European Tour for seven straight years (1993–99). When he chips, he picks the exact spot on the green where he wants the ball to land before it rolls toward the hole.

How the pros got started

Calvin Peete, who played on the PGA Tour in the 1970s and 1980s, was one of 19 children. His family didn't have extra money for golf clubs. When he was little, he broke his arm. It didn't heal properly, and he could not straighten it out. But when he was 23, Calvin decided he wanted to be a good golfer. With lots of practice and determination, he reached his goal. Once Calvin was good enough to play on the PGA Tour, he earned $2 million!

Chi Chi Rodriguez started to play golf using a stick and a round stone when he was a little boy in Puerto Rico. Now in his sixties, Chi Chi still plays golf and has raised more than $4 million to help kids who can't afford it to play golf.

Babe Zaharias played every sport when she was young, from boxing to tennis. When she was 18, she won three medals for the U.S. in track and field at the 1932 Olympic Games. Babe started playing golf when she was 21 and won the second tournament she played in! In only eight years on the Ladies Professional Golf Association (LPGA) tour, she won 31 tournaments and 10 major titles.

In 1932, when Arnold Palmer was just 3 years old, his father made him his own set of clubs. As a teenager, Arnold worked as a caddie at the Latrobe Country Club in Pennsylvania, where his father was the head professional and greens superintendent. He played golf whenever he could, pretending he was in a big tournament, beating all the great players. That's exactly what Arnold did when he got older! Arnold is now known as "the King" in the golf world.

Tiger Woods picked up his first golf club when he started walking. At the age of 2, he shot 48 for nine holes. Tiger's father, Earl, made sure he received the best instruction possible. Tiger won 3 U.S. Junior championships in a row and then 3 straight U.S. Amateurs. He joined the PGA Tour in 1996, when he was 20. The next year, Tiger won 4 tournaments, including the Masters. He won it by 12 shots — setting a new course record and becoming the youngest player to win that famous tournament.

Heroes of the past

Years ago, no one thought a golfer could win the four tournaments that used to make up golf's Grand Slam — the British Open, the British Amateur, the U.S. Open and the U.S. Amateur — in the same year. But Bobby Jones did just that in 1930. To win today's Grand Slam, a player must win all four major tournaments — the Masters, the British Open, the U.S. Open and the PGA Championship — to measure up to what Bobby did. Here are a few more of golf's heroes.

Ben Hogan was one of the best ball strikers in the history of golf. After he became a pro, he was in a terrible car accident. Doctors thought he would never walk again. But Ben was tough — and determined. He got better and went on to win the U.S. Open and the Masters. When pro golfers are hitting the ball really well, they say, "I hit it like Hogan."

Arnold Palmer may be the most famous golfer of all time. He won more than 90 tournaments around the world, including 8 major championships. Arnold, who is a renowned golf course designer as well, was the first golfer to earn more than $1 million in his career. He has had 17 holes in one.

Nancy Lopez began golfing in 1965, when she was 8. Four years later, she won the New Mexico State Women's Amateur Championship. After college, she joined LPGA Tour and won 9 tournaments in only her second year as a pro. Nancy still plays on the LPGA Tour.

Canadian Marlene Stewart Streit was the only woman golfer to win the Canadian Ladies' Amateur Championship and the British, Australian and U.S. Women's Amateur Championships. Later, she won the U.S. and Canadian Senior Women's Championships. Marlene also started a fund to help young female golfers improve their game and their education.

Jack Nicklaus, perhaps the greatest golfer of them all, started to play in 1950, when he was 10 years old. It was obvious even then that there was something special about this young golfer. The biggest clue? He shot 51 for nine holes — a great score! By 1986, Jack had won the Masters 6 times. During his career, he won 70 times on the PGA Tour.

Stars of today and tomorrow

Greg Norman was a teenager living in Australia when he discovered the book *Golf My Way,* written by Jack Nicklaus. He read the book over and over and practiced every day. In only a few years, he earned a reputation worldwide as a great golfer. "The Shark," as Greg is nicknamed, always draws a crowd to watch him play. He has won more than 70 tournaments worldwide.

Ernie Els is a big, tall man with a smooth and easy — but powerful — swing. That's why this South African's nickname is "the Big Easy." In 1997, he won his second U.S. Open, becoming only the second non-American to do so in 87 years. Ernie has won more than 30 tournaments around the world.

Se Ri Pak, of South Korea, didn't start playing until she was 14 years old. Only six years later in 1998, she won the U.S. Women's Open Championship and the McDonald's LPGA Championship. Se Ri says her father, who was a national amateur champion, helped her the most because he made her practice all the time as a teenager. Se Ri will be a player to watch for many years.

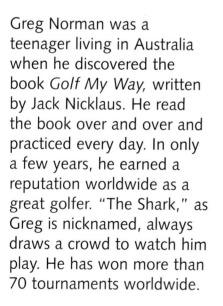

Tiger Woods was a legend even before he joined the 1996 PGA Tour at the age of 20. In 1997, he won the Masters by a record 12 strokes. By the end of 1999, he had won six straight PGA Tour tournaments, including the PGA Championship. He then won the 2000 U.S. Open by 15 strokes and the British Open by 8 strokes. This gave him what pro golfers call the "career Grand Slam," meaning he had won all four major championships in his lifetime. He was the youngest ever to do this. The final major championship that year was the PGA Championship, which Tiger had won in 1999. He won in 2000, too — the first time anyone had won two PGA Championships in a row since 1937.

LPGA pro Annika Sorenstam was 12 years old when she began golfing in Sweden in 1982. She got a lot of help from her parents and her sister, Lotta, who also went on to play on the LPGA Tour in the United States. Annika was the rookie of the year when she joined the LPGA in 1994. She has won many times since then, including the U.S. Women's Open Championship in 1995 and 1996.

David Duval was a great college player at Georgia Tech. People thought he would win everything when he turned pro, but it didn't work out that way. It took David 93 tries before he won his first tournament on the PGA Tour, but he then became one of the top players by winning 3 events in a row. In the 1999 Bob Hope Classic, David shot a 59 in the final round to win the tournament.

Tournaments and trophies

There are thousands of golf tournaments around the world every year, from the junior championship at your local golf course to the multimillion-dollar professional tours. But the most famous tournaments are the championships called the majors. There are four PGA majors — the Masters, the British Open, the U.S. Open and the PGA Championship. The LPGA also has four majors — the U.S. Women's Open Championship, the McDonald's LPGA Championship, the Nabisco Championship and the du Maurier Classic.

The Masters

The Masters is held every April at Augusta National Golf Club in Georgia. The course was originally designed in 1933 by Bobby Jones, the owner of the property and one of the best golfers of all time, and Alister Mackenzie, an architect who helped Bobby figure out the best places for each hole. Two years later, Bobby invited some friends who were great golfers to play with him in a tournament at his new course. The Masters was born!

AMAZING FACT

Only five players have ever won all four PGA majors in their lifetime — Tiger Woods, Jack Nicklaus, Gary Player, Ben Hogan and Gene Sarazen.

Annika Sorenstam at the 1999 McDonald's LPGA Championship

Nancy Lopez at the 1999 Nabisco Championship

The British Open

The British Open was first played in 1860 on a 12-hole golf course in Scotland called Old Prestwick. It is the oldest major championship. "Old Tom" Morris and his son, "Young Tom" Morris, won the Open eight times between them in the first 12 years it was held. The British Open moves to a different course in Scotland or England every year.

The U.S. Open

The U.S. Open was held for the first time in 1895. It is put on by the United States Golf Association for the best golfers in the world. One of the greatest stories about the U.S. Open is from 1913. That was when a 20-year-old amateur golfer and caddie named Francis Ouimet beat two of the best golfers from England, Harry Vardon and Ted Ray, to win the tournament.

The PGA Championship

The first PGA Championship was played in 1916, the same year the PGA of America was formed for golf professionals working at golf courses. The PGA wanted a tournament to determine the best golf pro in the United States. Now the PGA Championship is open to the best players from every country.

Tiger Woods was so happy he won the PGA Championship in 1999 that he kissed the trophy!

Golf collectibles

 Golf has been around for hundreds of years. That means there are all kinds of golf-related collectibles. Some collectibles cost only a few dollars, but others are very expensive. In 1998, owners of Spain's Valderrama Golf Course paid U.S. $175 000 for a putter made in the late 1700s or early 1800s. Antique golf balls are hard to find, but you may get one from the 1930s for about U.S. $50.

You don't have to collect antiques or spend a lot of money to be a golf collector. You can start a collection of bag tags and scorecards from the courses you've played on. Some people also collect ball markers, pencils, bag towels, hats or tees.

If you go to a golf tournament, you can collect autographs of famous golfers as well. Stand near the practice green, driving range or scoring tent and politely ask your favorite players for an autograph as they leave.

Selection of early golf clubs

Collection of golf tees

Great and goofy golf

Nothing stops great golfers like Se Ri Pak from making a shot!

• The lowest score for 18 holes in a tournament is 59. Several players have done that.

• American Floyd Rood made 114 737 strokes when he golfed across the United States, a distance of 5468 km (3398 mi.), in 1964. He lost 3511 balls!

• In 1987, James Carvill of Ireland played a full-length 18-hole course in only 27 minutes. It takes most people 4, 5 or even 6 hours!

• U.S. astronaut Alan Shepard is the only person who has hit a golf ball on the moon. He did it in 1969.

• In 1999, Canadian Jason Zuback won his fourth-straight World Long-Drive Championship. His longest drive ever was 511 yards. *The Guinness Book of Records* says American Michael Hoke Austin hit the longest drive in competition — 515 yards — in 1974. But there was a big wind behind him!

• The youngest golfer to have a hole in one is 4-year-old Scott Statler of the United States. The oldest is 99 years, 244 days old — Otto Bucher of Switzerland.

• Canadian Arthur Thompson shot a score of 103 in 1973. Nothing special, right? Except he did it when he was 103 years old!

• Canadian pro Rob McGregor holds the world record for bouncing a golf ball off a club — 5172 times.

• Worth Delton didn't know his ball had hit the cup of the 125-yard 7th hole at Tripoli Country Club in Milwaukee, U.S. — until he heard the cheers. Delton is a blind golfer!

Great moments

There are many great moments in a game that is more than 500 years old. Here are a few of the most important events in golf:

1457	Golf is mentioned in writing for the first time when the Scottish government outlaws it
1552	St. Andrews, the oldest and most famous golf course, is established in Scotland
1744	The first rules of golf are written down in Scotland
1860	Willie Park wins the first British Open
1873	Royal Montreal Golf Club, the first in North America, is founded
1895	Horace Rawlins wins the first U.S. Open
1904	George Lyon of Canada wins the gold medal in golf at the St. Louis Olympic Games — the last time golf was in the Olympics
1916	Jim Barnes wins the first U.S. PGA Championship
1930	Bobby Jones wins the Grand Slam — the British Open and Amateur Championships and the U.S. Open and Amateur Championships
1934	Horton Smith wins the first Masters Championship
1945	Byron Nelson wins 19 professional tournaments, including 11 in a row

1950	The Ladies Professional Golf Association (LPGA) is founded in the United States
1961	Players of color are allowed to golf in U.S. PGA tournaments
1968	The modern PGA Tour is formed in the United States
1977	Al Geiberger is the first to shoot 59 in a PGA Tour event
1978	Nancy Lopez wins 9 LPGA tournaments, including five in a row
1981	Kathy Whitworth is the first woman player to win $1 million in her career
1986	Pat Bradley wins 5 LPGA events, including 3 of the 4 majors
1989	The first golf course opens in the former Soviet Union
1990	Left-hander Phil Mickelson wins the U.S. Amateur and the National Collegiate Athletic Association (NCAA) Championship, the first player to do so since Jack Nicklaus in 1961
1991	Greg Norman wins his second British Open
1997	At 21, Tiger Woods becomes the youngest player to win Masters
1999	The first World Golf Championships are played, each with a total purse of $5 million
2000	At 24, Tiger wins three of the four major championships in the same year, the first man to do so since Ben Hogan in 1953. He soon became the youngest man to complete a career Grand Slam, winning all four major championships in his lifetime.

Golf talk

ace: a hole in one

address: the position you take when you are ready to hit the ball

away: the player whose ball is farthest from the hole is said to be away

birdie: getting the ball in the hole in one stroke under par (taking three strokes on a par-four hole, for example)

bogey: getting the ball in the hole in one stroke over par (taking five strokes on a par-four hole, for example). A double-bogey would be two over par, a triple-bogey three over par, and so on.

bunker: a large sand-filled area, also called a sand trap

chip: a short shot from just off the green

divot: a hole in the grass made by your club when you hit the ball

dogleg: a fairway that curves left (dogleg left) or right (dogleg right) from where you tee off to the hole. Often you can't see the flag on a dogleg because it is around the bend in the fairway.

eagle: getting the ball in the hole in two strokes under par (taking two strokes on a par-four hole, for example)

fairway: the area between the teeing ground and the green, except for the rough and hazards

fore: the warning word you shout if your ball is headed toward another person

green: the putting area with very short grass where the hole is located

handicap: a method of adding or subtracting strokes to allow players of all levels to compete fairly with one another

hazard: any bunker or water hazard (creek, pond, lake, etc.)

honor: the person who had the lowest score on the previous hole is said to have the honor and tees off first on the next hole

hook: a golf shot that curves sharply to the left (for a right-handed player)

marking your ball: when you put a small coin or similar marker behind your ball on the green. You can then pick up and clean your ball. Make sure you put it back in the same place when you are ready to putt.

match play: when each hole is a separate contest. For example, if you take four shots on the first hole and I take five, you win it and are up one hole. If, on the next hole, you have six and I have five, I win the hole and the match is even. The player who wins the most holes during the round wins the match.

mulligan: when you get to take a bad shot over. Experienced golfers don't do this because the rules do not allow it and it slows play.

par: the number of strokes it should take a good golfer to play a hole, allowing for two putts on the green. (For example, on a par five, a player should take three shots to get to the green and two putts to put the ball in the hole.)

penalty stroke: if you do something wrong — such as lose your ball or hit someone else's ball — you must add one or two strokes to your score. These are called penalty strokes.

rough: the longer grass that lines each side of the fairway

slice: a golf shot that curves sharply to the right (for a right-handed player)

stroke: any attempt to hit the ball. Even if you miss, or whiff, it — you have taken a stroke.

stroke play: when you count one stroke each time you hit the ball (or try to hit it). After the round, you add up the strokes you made, plus any penalty strokes. The player with the lowest total wins the round.

tee: the short wooden peg on which you place the ball when starting each hole. Also, the area where the tee markers are located.

George Lyon won a gold medal in golf at the 1904 Olympics

Index

Photo credits

Cover Photo Credits

Model photo (front and back cover): Ray Boudreau

Background photo (front and back cover): Frank Baldassara

Left inset photo (front cover): Future Links

Right inset photo (front cover): Frank Baldassara

Abbreviations:

t = top; b = bottom; c = center; l = left; r = right

Future Links = Courtesy Future Links Program

RCGA = Courtesy Royal Canadian Golf Association/Canadian Golf Hall of Fame Archives

p. 4: (l, r) Future Links; **p. 5:** (t) Future Links, (b) Mike Powell/Allsport; **p. 6:** Bell Canadian Open Collection/RCGA; **p. 7:** RCGA; **p. 8:** RCGA; **p. 10:** (t, b) Doug Ball; **p. 11:** (tl) Doug Ball, (tc, tr, br) RCGA, (bl) Courtesy MJ Miller Advertising; **p. 12:** (t) Courtesy MJ Miller Advertising, (b) Future Links; **p. 13:** (all) RCGA; **p. 14:** (all) Doug Ball; **p. 15:** Bob Daemmrich Photo, Inc.; **p. 16:** Doug Ball; **p. 17:** Doug Ball; **p. 19:** Craig Jones/Allsport; **p. 21:** (t) Bell Canadian Open Collection/RCGA, (b) Future Links; **p. 22:** Doug Ball; **p. 23:** Doug Ball; **p. 24:** Future Links; **p. 25:** Future Links; **p. 26:** Future Links; **p. 27:** (t,b) Doug Ball; **p. 29:** (t) Brooks Dodge/New England Stock, (b) Courtesy Andrea Lyon-Kewley, Junior Director, Yellowknife, NT, Yellowknife Golf Club; **p. 30:** (l) RCGA, (r) Bell Canadian Open Collection/RCGA; **p. 31:** (l) Andrew Redington/Allsport, (r) RCGA, (b) Jonathan Ferrey/Allsport; **p. 32:** (l) RCGA, (c) Andy Lyons/Allsport, (b) United States Golf Association; **p. 33:** (t) RCGA, (b) Jon Ferrey/Allsport; **p. 34:** (t,b) RCGA; **p. 35:** (tl, b) RCGA, (tr) Harry How/Allsport; **p. 36:** (l) Stephen Munday/Allsport, (c) Jon Ferrey/Allsport, (r) Andrew Redington/Allsport; **p. 37:** (l) Clive Mason/Allsport, (c) Stephen Munday/Allsport, (r) Bell Canadian Open Collection/RCGA; **p. 38:** (l) Andrew Redington/Allsport, (r) Harry How/Allsport; **p. 39:** Craig Jones/Allsport; **p. 40:** (l,r) RCGA; **p. 41:** Craig Jones/Allsport; **p. 45:** RCGA.

Illustration credit

Illustrations © Greg Douglas 2000. Illustrations first appeared in *Future Links Junior Golf Program Student Guidebook: Level 1.*

Property of the
TOWN OF GRANBY, CONN.
F. H. COSSITT LIBRARY

Return to
CHILDREN'S ROOM
F. H. COSSITT LIBRARY